real U®

GUIDE TO

IDENTITY THEFT

FRANK W. ABAGNALE

WITH JOHANNA BODNYK

Real U Guides

Publisher and CEO:
Steve Schultz

Editor-in-Chief:
Megan Stine

Art Director:
C.C. Krohne

Designer:
David Jackson

Illustration:
Mike Strong

Production Manager:
Alice Todd

Library of Congress Control Number: 2004094759

ISBN: 1-932999-01-9

First Edition
10 9 8 7 6 5 4 3 2 1

Published by
Real U, Inc.
2582 Centerville Rosebud Rd.
Loganville, GA 30052

www.realuguides.com

Real U is a registered trademark of Real U, Inc.

Photo Credits:
Cover and Page 1: Megan Stine; Page 3: Adri Berger/Getty Images; Page 4:
Man and woman, Digital Vision/Getty Images; Mail sign, ArtToday; Page
5: Document being shredded, James Darrell/Getty Images; Man at key-
board, ArtToday; Page 6: Digital Vision/Getty Images; Page 8: Abagnale &
Associates; Page 9: Megan Stine; Page 10: Keith Brofsky; Page 11: Megan
Stine; Page 12: Nick Koudis/Getty Images; Page 14: ArtToday; Page 15:
ArtToday; Page 16: Bart Geerliqs/Getty Images; Page 18: ArtToday; Page
19: ArtToday; Page 20: ArtToday; Page 21: ArtToday; Page 22: ArtToday;
Page 23: Digital Vision/Getty Images; Page 24: Digital Vision/Getty Images;
Page 27: ArtToday; Page 28: ArtToday; Page 29: ArtToday; Page 30:
ArtToday; Page 32: ArtToday; Page 33: Card in slot, ArtToday; People at
bar, ArtToday; Page 34: ArtToday; Page 35: ArtToday; Page 36: James
Darrell/Getty Images; Page 37: Tony Anderson/Getty Images; Page 39:
Vicky Kasala/Getty Images; Page 40: ArtToday; Page 42: Nancy R.
Cohen/Getty Images; Page 43: Ken Usami/Getty Images; Page 44: Ghislain
& Marie de Lossy/Getty Images; Page 45: ArtToday; Page 46: ArtToday;
Page 48: Photodisc Collection/Getty Images; Page 49: ArtToday; Page 50:
Barry Rosenthal/Getty Images; Page 51: ArtToday; Page 52: ArtToday;
Page 53: ArtToday; Page 55: Don Farrall/Getty Images; Page 56: Digital
Vision/Getty Images; Page 57: Past Due background, Ryan McVay/Getty
Images; Passport, Megan Stine; Page 58: ArtToday; Page 59: ArtToday;
Page 60: Megan Stine; Page 61: Photodisc Collection/Getty Images; Page
63: ArtToday; Back cover: Megan Stine.

realU

GUIDE TO
IDENTITY
THEFT

FRANK W. ABAGNALE

WITH JOHANNA BODNYK

GUIDE TO IDENTITY THEFT
TABLE OF CONTENTS

GUIDE TO

IDENTITY THEFT

You don't want to be a victim....

Remember the kid in elementary school who was always picked last for kickball? The one who might as well have had, "Beat me, steal my lunch money," written in big letters across the front of his T-shirts? When bullies spotted that kid, the results were never pretty.

Well, identity thieves are the new bullies on the playground, and they're after a lot more than your lunch money. Specifically, they're after your personal information—Social Security numbers, credit card numbers, even just your name and date of birth—so they can use it for fraud or theft. And more than just cornering you behind the tire swings, identity thieves can create a whole world of pain when they use your personal information to max out your credit cards, drain your bank accounts, or apply for loans in your name.

Identity theft is the fastest growing criminal activity in the U.S.—but there are ways to protect yourself from it, and there are strategies for coping if you find yourself getting picked on.

So don't be that kid on the playground with the dorky glasses. Toss out the "Beat Me" T-shirt and read on to learn how you can get tough with identity thieves, and avoid the #1 crime in America.

And welcome to realU

MEET FRANK ABAGNALE

CATCH ME THEN

If you've seen the movie about my life starring Leo DiCaprio, or read my autobiography *Catch Me If You Can*, you probably already know the basic facts about my early life—about how, between the ages of 16 and 21, I began what was to become one of the most daring and amazing adventures in stolen identity the world has ever seen. For those few short years, I lived an incredible life of luxury—flying all over the world, wining and dining beautiful women, dressing in the best clothes, and living in the most expensive hotels. I supported this lifestyle by cashing more than 2.5 million dollars' worth of fraudulent checks. I also forged documents that allowed me to pose successfully as a Pan Am pilot, a doctor, a lawyer, and a college professor. So when I tell you I know a lot about identity theft, I'm not exaggerating. I know exactly how an identity thief thinks from the inside out—because I've been one myself.

CATCH ME NOW

I'm not proud of the things I did when I was young, but I am proud of the way I've been able to turn my life of crime into a life of great personal satisfaction as a teacher and consultant at the FBI Academy, as a consultant to the banking industry and corporations worldwide, and as a highly sought after authority in the areas of forgery, embezzlement and document security.

How did I manage the transformation? In the early years, it wasn't easy. Of course I was caught and arrested for my crimes, and served time in prison—6 months in a French prison followed by 6 months in a Swedish prison and then 4 years in a U.S. Federal

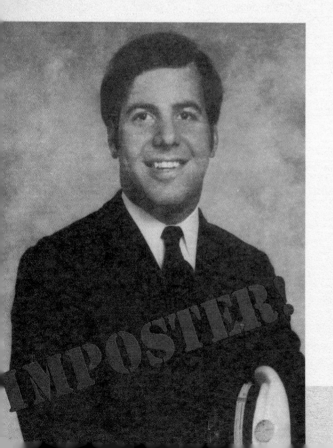

Frank–2004

prison. The European prisons nearly broke my soul but the U.S. prison term gave me time to grow up, study, earn my GED, and think about the kind of life I wanted to have when I came out.

Finally, I was paroled and given the chance I'd been hoping for. But my status as an ex-con provided very limited opportunities—in a pizza parlor, then a supermarket. But no matter how reliable I was, no matter how much of a model employee, when my employers found out about my criminal past I was fired.

I had come out of prison wanting to prove that I could lead a clean life and make a contribution to society. Imagine how demoralizing it was when I realized that I was never going to be trusted again. I was on the verge of giving up hope when an idea came to me. Why not put my past to good use by offering my expertise to banks, law enforcement officials, and corporations? After all, no one knew as much about forging checks and faking identities as I did.

I approached a bank and made them a deal: I would come in and make a presentation about fraud prevention to their employees. If they didn't find my advice useful, they didn't have to pay me a dime. But if they liked what they heard, they would pay me $500 and recommend my services to other banks and businesses in the area.

That was the beginning of what has become a very rewarding career. For the past 30 years, I've been advising banks, corporations, and law enforcement agencies about how to thwart forgery and fraud. I've developed patents for security techniques that are used on millions of payroll checks and bank documents nationwide. I also teach regularly at the FBI Academy and lecture at FBI field offices around the country—but those services are always offered gratis, for no pay.

And the best part of the story? I've made more money through these honest endeavors than I ever made by committing fraud.

Turn the page to learn more about how I help prevent identity theft every day ⟶

Is your ATM secure?

TRICKS OF THE TRADE: HOW I HELP PREVENT ID THEFT

PAY DAY

Have you ever noticed a small red circle on the back of your payroll check? Rub it, and it seems to disappear, but only temporarily. A few moments later, the red ink will reappear, proving that you're holding an authentic ADP paycheck. That's a security feature called thermochromatic ink, which I helped develop in tandem with a team of technology specialists. It's just one of many security features I've come up with to help thwart check forgers. See if you can find one of my favorite security features on a paycheck in your possession—the micro-printing that reveals my signature so small you'll need a magnifying glass to read it.

If you get a paycheck every two weeks, there's a good chance you've handled a document I designed. You may also carry a credit card with security features I implemented or use ATM machines that I tested and foiled—which were then redesigned based on my suggestions for making them more secure.

Here's a quick look at only some of the strategies that I've helped develop to make identity theft more difficult.

THE SUPERCHECK

One way to make sure your checking account doesn't become a target for forgers is to make sure you always order your checks directly from the bank. Bank checks have more security features than checks ordered from a catalog or online. But an even better way to secure your checking account is to use the Supercheck that I designed. These checks come with a whole array of security features including a watermark, thermochromatic ink, chemicallyreactive paper, and UV light-sensitive ink and fibers. Is it overkill to use these checks for your household account? That depends on how much you have to protect, and how much hassle you're willing to put up with if someone writes a bad check in your name.

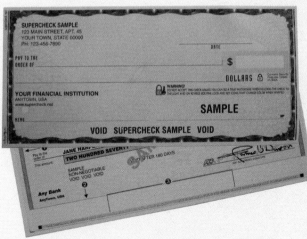

WATCH OUT

If you happen to be one of the people who can afford to buy a $15,000 watch, you want to know that the timepiece you're getting is the real thing, not a fake. Watch manufacturers have a similar agenda, in that they don't

want counterfeiters to rip off their designs and pass inferior products off to an unsuspecting public. I designed a security feature that is inscribed on every watch case for a certain luxury watchmaker—a form of micro-printing that can only be seen under a high magnification lens. It's one small step in the fight against counterfeit merchandise, a huge multi-billion dollar industry.

EYES WIDE OPEN

One of the best strategies I use in my own life is a strategy everyone can put into place—and that is to make sure you don't set yourself up as an easy mark. For example, I never purchase merchandise on the Internet—it's a risk I just don't want to take. And I have an elaborate system of lights and security cameras around my house—at night the place is lit up like a football field. It's my way of letting people know that I'm paying attention, that if they're looking for an easy target they'd better look somewhere else. You may not want to surround your house with a security system on a par with the one at Fort Knox, but there are many things you can easily do to thwart the hundreds and thousands of identity thieves who are just waiting to pick their next victims.

Read on! ⟶

IDENTITY THEFT

101

A Real U
Crash
Course

Identity theft, that nasty crime in which someone obtains and uses your personal information to commit fraud or theft, is the fastest growing criminal activity in the U.S. And it could be coming soon to a bank account near you!

You've probably heard about the most common forms of identity theft—when a thief tracks down your credit card numbers, and then uses them to max out your accounts. That kind of theft—the stolen credit card variety—is fairly easy to notice and fix.

Things get more complicated, though, when a thief steals your SSN from records at your job and uses it to apply for a mortgage or car loan. Cases like this are hard to detect and often even harder to resolve.

The problem is that all the techno-marvels we take for granted often help to serve up our identities on a silver platter to clever, techno-savvy thieves. For example, it's great to be able to shop online, but your electronic transaction may give a hacker access to your credit card number. And while preapproved credit applications make it easier for you to get a card, they also make it a breeze for an imposter to get credit using your name.

Your personal information is available in more places than you may even realize—and it presents thieves with the perfect opportunities to make some quick cash.

10 WAYS THIEVES STEAL YOUR INFO

1 SNATCHING YOUR PURSE OR WALLET

Pickpockets and purse snatchers are going about it the old-fashioned way. Not particularly inspired, but very effective.

2 STEALING YOUR MAIL

There's a rich bounty of information in the form of credit card statements, new checks, and that unending stream of preapproved credit offers in your mailbox. And it's not just snail mail. Your electronic communications are vulnerable to theft as well.

3 DUMPSTER DIVING

No, not the latest extreme sport, just a profitable if rather messy way to get your private info from your trash. Your old computer can also yield some great stuff to a crook with a few techno-skills.

4 BREAKING INTO YOUR HOUSE OR YOUR COMPUTER

Cyber-thieves are eager to steal that file you labeled "Important Private Confidential Sensitive Personal Information." Subtlety's not your strong point, is it?

5 CONNING A CREDIT BUREAU

By posing as someone legit, like a bank or an employer, thieves can obtain all your vital stats in one handy package. Don't let them order your report before you do! (See Page 23 for the details on credit reports.)

6 EAVESDROPPING AND SHOULDER SURFING

Some thieves try to listen in on your conversations or watch you enter your PIN at an ATM, using high-tech Bond gear like binoculars and video cameras (although probably without the sexy British accent).

You don't have to tattoo your Social Security number on your forehead and lend your credit card to random strangers to become a victim of identity theft. Determined crooks have come up with some pretty sneaky ways to get your digits. Here's a thoroughly depressing look at how they do it.

7 SKIMMING

By running your plastic through a bogus reader designed to copy the card number, your seemingly innocent Food Mart guy or friendly waitress just might be ripping you off.

8 PRETEXTING, PHISHING, SCAMMING, AND SPOOFING

Four fancy ways of saying, "playing you for a fool." By mail, telephone, or e-mail, thieves pretend to be from businesses with actual reasons for needing your SSN and mother's maiden name. As if you didn't already hate telemarketers enough!

9 INSIDE JOB

Sadly, a significant amount of identity theft is perpetrated by family members or relatives, who have easy access to your records. Employees and co-workers can also get your personal information at work.

10 STEALING FROM COMPANIES

A large number of businesses have you in their database systems, along with all the information a thief could want. To get the goods on you, thieves hack into databases, steal physical files, or pay employees to divulge your data.

TO EARN SOME EXTRA SNEAKINESS POINTS,

a thief can also fill out a "change of address form" for you so the evidence of his crime won't wind up on your doorstep. Lazier thieves may simply buy your information from someone who has used one of the above methods. That's bad news, since it means multiple imposters may be committing fraud in your name.

WHAT THEY DO WITH **YOUR INFO**

identity theft victim

Once they've got your data, thieves can use it in a lot of different ways. The most common kind of fraud occurs when crooks go on a spending spree to rack up charges on your existing credit card account—but the fun doesn't stop there!

- They use your credit card or credit card number to charge purchases to your accounts, often changing the address your bills are sent to so you won't notice right away.

- Using your name, date of birth, and Social Security number, a thief can open a new credit card account in your name.

- With the same info, crooks can apply for phone or wireless service.

- Some thieves use your name to open a bank account and write bad checks. Others counterfeit your checks or steal your debit card number to drain your existing bank account.

- Your identity can be quite handy when a thief wants to take out car loans or mortgages.

- Crooks can use your name when filing for bankruptcy, or co-opt your entire identity to hide a bad credit history or a criminal record and start a "new life."

- Theives can use your name and Social Security number to get a job, and taxes will be deducted from their paychecks in your name. When you fail to report that income, the IRS could think that you're filing a fraudulent tax return.

- In rare cases, a thief might give your name to police when arrested. When he's a no-show at his hearing, guess who the cops are coming after with a warrant?

HOW **YOU** LOSE

Believe it or not, if your identity is stolen, the chances are about 50/50 that you'll never find out exactly how it happened. Some kinds of theft—when a crook steals data from company files, for instance—are very hard for victims to trace.

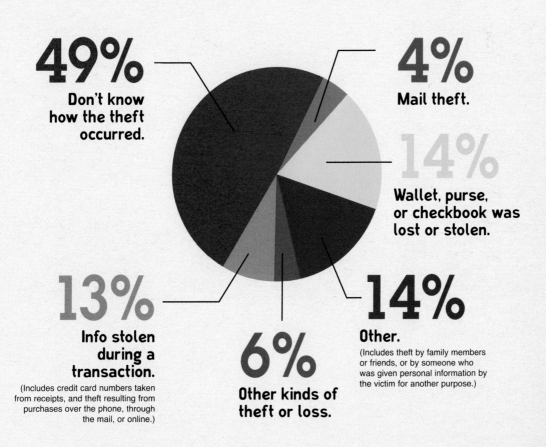

49%
Don't know how the theft occurred.

4%
Mail theft.

14%
Wallet, purse, or checkbook was lost or stolen.

13%
Info stolen during a transaction.
(Includes credit card numbers taken from receipts, and theft resulting from purchases over the phone, through the mail, or online.)

6%
Other kinds of theft or loss.

14%
Other.
(Includes theft by family members or friends, or by someone who was given personal information by the victim for another purpose.)

MORE BAD —

Many people have been told that the banks and credit card companies are the "real victims."

THE IMPACT ON VICTIMS

In the search for help and sympathy, too many identity theft victims run into the ridiculous attitude that they aren't really victims at all. Many people have been told that the banks and credit card companies (who lose tens of thousands of dollars per incident) are the "real victims." Although it's true that most individuals don't end up paying for the fraudulent charges, having your identity stolen is no walk in the park. Getting debt collectors off your back and straightening out your credit history can be a long hard struggle. And even after the theft itself is stopped, victims are sometimes denied loans, housing, and employment because of bad credit. Try telling someone who's spent hundreds of hours clearing her name (and hundreds of dollars in expenses) that she isn't a victim! For more on the emotional impact of identity theft, see Page 45.

FRIGHTENING
FACTS & FIGURES

- In 2002, an estimated 3.25 million Americans discovered that they were victims of the more complicated form of identity theft, in which new accounts are opened in the victim's name.

- Including the simpler kind of identity theft, where only existing credit cards are used, 10 million Americans found out that they were victims in 2002.

- Between 1990 and 2003, 33 million people, or one in six Americans, became victims of identity theft.

- The Federal Trade Commission's Identity Theft Hotline receives 5,000 calls a week.

- The average identity theft victim spends $500 dealing with identity theft. When a "new account" is opened in the victim's name, the average cost to clean up the mess rises to $1,200.

- 27% of "new account" victims spend 6 months or more clearing their names. On average, such victims devote 60 hours to resolving the problems the theft creates.

- Nearly 50% of victims have no idea how their identities were stolen.

- Only 11% of victims are aware that their personal information has been stolen before they discover evidence of fraud.

- 18% of "new account" victims know who stole their identity—because it was a relative or a member of their own family.

> **10 MILLION AMERICANS WERE VICTIMS OF IDENTITY THEFT IN 2002.**

ID THEFT

You May Already Be A Winner!

The scene: after searching for what seems like forever, you've finally found the perfect car. Or your dream house. Or that too-good-to-be-true job with five weeks vacation and a six-figure salary. All you need to do is fill out the paperwork, talk to the right people, go through the motions, and it's yours.

Didn't get the job.

But you've got to move quickly, because a deal like this is bound to be gone in the blink of an eye. The twist: You do everything right…but your loan application is turned down…or inexplicably, you don't get the job. What happened? Someone turned up a bad credit report.

If you think your credit is fine, think again. Do you know for sure? Have you taken a look at your credit report lately? Here's a sobering fact: many identity theft victims don't know they are victims until they apply for a loan, a job, or something else requiring a credit check. And of course that's the worst time to find out.

4 WARNING SIGNS

If your identity is stolen you need to know about it ASAP so you can stop further fraud and work on repairing your good name. Here are some major signs that you are the victim of identity theft.

1 DENIED!

Your application for credit or a job is turned down based on your credit report—and as far as you know, your credit history is good.

2 RIPPED OFF!

Your credit card, bank balance, or other financial statements show charges you never made. Or you receive a statement for a credit card you didn't know you had.

3 HARASSED!

Collections agencies start calling you out of the blue to collect on debts you never incurred.

4 MISSING MAIL.

This one might seem the most innocent—you might even be grateful at first! But if your bills stop coming, that's a bad thing. It might mean an identity thief has changed your address on your credit card statement so you won't notice the fraudulent charges on your account. And guess what? The thief isn't taking care of those bills for you.

If you have one of these symptoms, don't assume it's simply a clerical error, and don't put off investigating it. Find out what's up. Your first move? Order your credit report and see for yourself what the deal is. See Page 26 to learn more about this crucial step.

BIG

BAD CREDIT REPORTS

Credit bureaus—or credit reporting agencies—are in the business of being nosy about how quickly and reliably you pay your bills. Although the name "credit bureau" sounds somewhat official, these agencies aren't non-profit organizations or goverment bureaus.

They're in it for the dough, just like everyone else. Credit bureaus make their money by selling the information on your credit report to businesses such as banks, savings and loans, credit unions, finance companies, and retailers—who use the info to decide whether they want to issue you credit.

Our credit report was ok!

A LOOK

AT YOUR CREDIT REPORT

Your credit report reveals a surprising amount of information including:

- ☐ Your name, address, SSN, and employment information.

- ☐ What credit accounts have been opened in your name, and the current status of those accounts—whether they are active or closed, for instance.

- ☐ The balance on each account, how much your monthly payments are, and whether or not you make those payments on time.

- ☐ What other companies have ordered your credit report in the past. These prior requests are called "inquiries."

- ☐ Your credit score, which determines your "creditworthiness." Your score is based on such things as whether you make payments promptly, how much credit you already have, and how long you've had various accounts. Creditors look at your credit score as a way to predict whether you will be able to pay your bills on time.

Does it all add up?

CREDIT MONITORING SERVICES OR DO-IT-YOURSELF?

How do they know so much?

Some of this information, your name and address, for instance, comes from public records. The majority of it, however, is reported to the credit bureaus by banks and other businesses that have issued you credit. These companies report to the credit bureaus on a monthly basis, telling them what your balance is and whether you've been keeping up your payments.

Creditors also let the credit bureaus know when you—or an identity thief using your information—open up a new credit account. So even if there are no other clues that your identity has been stolen, your credit report can tell you if someone has been obtaining credit in your name.

When you apply for any kind of credit— a car loan, let's say—the bank checks you out by ordering your credit report. Based on your credit history and score, the bank decides whether or not to approve your loan application. If an identity thief has been using your identity to open bogus accounts, those actions will show up on your credit report and negatively affect your credit score. (And guess what? Identity thieves don't tend to pay their bills on time...or at all. Big surprise.)

The result? The bank won't exactly be eager to lend you money. Now don't you want to know what's on that report?

You may have noticed that there's no shortage of companies that are eager to help you monitor your credit. The best of these services will monitor your credit on a daily basis and notify you that day by phone, e-mail, or even pager if anything smells fishy. A top-notch program will also monitor all 3 credit bureaus—Equifax, Experian, and TransUnion—not just one. Additional features may include identity theft insurance and help in resolving the problems if your identity is stolen. Be aware, however, that the insurance only covers the cost of repairing the problem —it doesn't cover your actual cash loss from the theft.

All 3 credit bureaus offer monitoring services, as do a number of private companies such as PrivacyGuard. The costs vary depending on the services provided, but daily credit monitoring averages about $120 per year. Yes, it's significantly more than you'd pay if you order your reports yourself a few times a year—but it also provides a lot more protection. The truth is that individuals simply can't keep track of potential assaults to their credit *on a daily basis* the way credit monitoring services can. And as for ordering the reports yourself, the big question is: will you? A reliable credit monitoring service can give you some peace of mind, knowing that someone else is keeping track of your credit every single day, making sure no new thefts have occurred. Even so, make sure you're dealing with a legitimate company before you sign up.

More about your credit report →

HOW TO GET YOUR CREDIT REPORT

There are three major credit bureaus in the U.S — Equifax, Experian, and TransUnion. If life were simple, your reports from Experian and Equifax would be identical. But they probably aren't.

To stay on top of your credit situation—and give yourself half a chance to catch identity theft as soon as it happens—you need to order a copy of your credit report once a year from each of the three major credit bureaus.

Wait a minute, you're thinking—once a year? Is that often enough? You're right—it's not. An identity thicf could do a lot of damage to your credit in twelve months, so to get more bang for your buck, it's a good idea to stagger your orders from the three different credit bureaus. Look at Equifax in January, TransUnion in May, and so on. If you notice anything suspicious one month, order the other two as well so you have all the information as soon as possible.

Why check all three?

Well, if life were simple, your reports from Experian, Equifax and TransUnion would be identical. But they probably aren't. The three bureaus may get different information, and there's likely to be a typo or two, just to keep things interesting. Also, when checking your creditworthiness, lenders might order your report from only one of the three bureaus. That means the signs of trouble—like the request a bank makes when a thief applies for a car loan in your name—will only appear on one of the three reports.

What's this going to cost me?

By federal law, the credit bureaus can charge you no more than nine dollars and change for each copy of your report. Some states have laws lowering the price for the first copy you order each year. (And if you live in Georgia, you lucky thing, you get two copies a year for free!) Check out the chart on Page 28 to find out if you're living in one of the discount states.

No matter where you live, you get a complimentary copy if you are unemployed and planning to apply for a job in the next six months, or if you have been turned down for a loan or a job because of a bad credit report. Identity theft victims also have the right to receive a free credit report from each bureau.

Not so free.

If you're online, you've probably seen a lot of offers for "free" credit reports. Watch out—this is a different story entirely. "Free" in this case means either, "we'll also enroll you in our credit-monitoring service and charge you an arm and a leg," or "we're actually identity thieves trying to con you into giving us your Social Security number." See the box on Page 25 for more on credit-monitoring services. To avoid a scam, never give out your personal information in response to an unsolicited e-mail.

Okay, what do I do?

You can order your credit report online, over the phone, or by mail. If you go online, you get to see your credit report instantly, but the process is a little tricky. Although the law says the credit bureaus have to give you your credit report for $9.00 or less, they'd much rather sell you additional services for more money. See the box on Page 26 for some insight into why you might choose a credit monitoring service. But if you decide you just want the basic report, you may have to click through a number of web pages to find it. Skip past the first more expensive options, and look around on the web site until you find the option that says something like "single credit report" or "$9.00 credit report."

Even harder to locate on the credit bureau web pages is the option for folks who get a free report because they are unemployed,

have been denied credit, or are identity theft victims. A cryptic reference, in gray fine print, will be hidden at the top, bottom, or sides of the screen. You might have to pull out your magnifying glass to find it.

Once you do, you'll learn that credit bureaus aren't required to give you a free report online. If you live in Georgia or are unemployed, for instance, they can still charge you nine bucks for an online credit report. To get your free or discounted report, you may have to order over the phone, or even by mail. So if you want a free report, skip the online option. The easiest way to find out how to order a freebie is to call each credit bureau and listen to the automated options.

ORDERING YOUR CREDIT REPORT

Equifax Information Services LLC
P.O. Box 740241
Atlanta, GA 30374
800-685-1111
www.equifax.com

Experian
P.O. Box 2002
Allen, TX 75013
888-397-3742
www.experian.com

TransUnion LLC
Consumer Disclosure Center
P.O. Box 1000
Chester, PA 19022
800-888-4213
www.transunion.com

*If you need to order by mail, it's a good idea to call first or go online so you know exactly what information to include in your request.

CREDIT REPORT PRICES BY STATE AND SITUATION

If you live in:	Your first copy from each bureau each year is:
Colorado, Maine, Maryland, Massachusetts, New Jersey, or Vermont	FREE!
Georgia	FREE, and so is your second copy each year!
California	$8.00*
Connecticut	$5.00*
Minnesota	$3.00*
Montana	$8.50*
U.S. Virgin Islands	$1.00*
All other states	$9.00*

*plus tax where applicable

Special Situations:	Your credit report, no matter where you live, is:
If you are unemployed and applying for a job in the next 6 months, or if you receive welfare assistance...	FREE!
If you have been turned down for credit, a job or anything else because of bad credit...	FREE!
If you are a victim of identity theft...	FREE!

DECIPHERING YOUR CREDIT REPORT

Okay, you got your credit reports, but oh dear...they don't seem to be written in English. Don't panic—you don't have to understand every detail to look for signs of identity theft. Here's what you need to check out:

☐ The "Applicant" and "File Variations" sections at the beginning of the report list your personal information. Look here for details that just don't click. If the date of birth is totally off or there's an address where you've never lived, that's a clue that someone who isn't you has been opening credit accounts in your name.

☐ Your report will also list "Aliases" and "Former Names"—make sure all of these are names you've actually used. (To simplify things and prevent errors, it's best to always use the exact same name when applying for credit. Make a choice now about your middle initial and stick to it.)

☐ Look closely at the "Credit History" section and check for accounts you don't recognize. For the accounts that are legitimately yours, make sure the number under the "Balance Owing" column jibes with what you've really spent.

☐ The "Inquiries" section tells you who has requested your credit report—something which is typically done before opening a credit account for you. If an identity thief got a credit card in your name, the credit card company will be listed here, on at least one of the reports. So look carefully for any inquiries you don't remember authorizing.

☐ Some quirks in your report may be the result of a clerical error rather than identity theft. Or an identity thief may be using your name and ID to get a loan, which he is then repaying promptly. Don't make the mistake of thinking that a good paying account is a benefit to your credit score. You could wind up being denied credit later on when the person suddenly defaults on "your" loan— or even simply because you now have too much credit! See Page 55 to find out how to dispute errors in your report.

PREVENTING

BOTTOM LINE:
NO ONE'S GOING TO
WATCH OUT FOR YOU,
SO YOU'VE GOT TO
DO IT YOURSELF.

IDENTITY THEFT

There's good news and there's bad news about preventing identity theft. The good news is that if you remain reasonably paranoid and moderately vigilant— and never mind that both of those terms are loaded with contradictions—you've got a halfway fighting chance of avoiding becoming a victim.

The bad news is that taking all the steps to prevent identity theft can begin to feel like a part-time job. By the time you're done ordering credit reports, shredding documents, and checking your credit card statement like an IRS auditor each month, you barely have time to enjoy the fact that your financial identity is still in good shape.

But hold on—there's more good news. The fact is, a part-time job guarding your financial identity is better than the full-time job of correcting the mess if the ID thieves make you a target. (See Page 47 for a heart-stopping description of the new full-time job many victims face.)

Bottom line: no one's going to watch out for you, so you've got to do it yourself. This chapter is filled with tips for lowering your risk and spotting some of the classic scams, plus one key piece of advice about something you *don't* need to do to protect yourself.

Read on.

20 Ways to Lower Your Risk

1. Check your credit reports every year!

We've said it once, and we'll say it again. Whether or not you have any of the identity theft symptoms described on Page 20, this step is absolutely vital. If an identity thief uses your SSN to open a new credit card account with a fake address and phone number, you may not find out about it until the damage is done—unless you check your credit report periodically.

2. Keep track of your billing cycles.

A missing bill doesn't mean that the credit card company is giving you a month off. It may mean a thief has changed your address. Call and figure out why they don't seem to want your money.

3. Examine your financial statements like an obsessed accountant.

As soon as a statement arrives, go over it carefully to make sure you really bought all that stuff. If you didn't, deal with it right away. (If you did, give yourself a moment to recover from the shock—you really bought all that stuff?)

4. Guard your mail from theft.

Pick it up as soon as the mailman puts it down—otherwise some well-meaning thief might figure you don't want it. When you order new checks, go get them yourself from the bank instead of having them mailed. And burn some extra calories by taking your outgoing mail to a drop box rather than leaving it in your mailbox. Does all that sound like too much trouble? A locked mailbox also does the trick nicely. If you live in a particularly high-crime area, consider playing it extra safe with a P.O. box. And finally, if you go on vacation, ask a neighbor to pick up your mail, or call the post office to have your mail held for you.

5. Invest in a shredder.

When chucking something sensitive, destroy it first. Cross-cut shredders dice your data into tiny squares instead of settling for strips like a traditional shredder. The cross-cut style is your safest bet, unless of course your identity thief really likes puzzles.

6. Avoid sketchy ATMs.

Some ATMs are set up to copy your bank card as well as give you money. Unless it's a dire emergency, steer clear of the "KaSh-O-RaMa" at the end of that dark alley.

7. Be suspicious of unexpected calls.

When a "business" calls or e-mails and asks for personal information, indulge in a little healthy paranoia. Make it a policy not to get personal unless you're the one who initiated the contact. Even if the caller seems legit, it's best to double-check. (See Page 38 for the low-down on scams.)

8. Put real passwords on your accounts.

Yeah, it's a hassle, and you might be tempted to use the same short and simple combination for each of your bank and service accounts. Keep in mind, though, that even the densest crook will eventually crack "1234," and believe it or not, your mother's maiden name is hardly a government secret. Use a strong password—a "random" eight-character combination of numbers, letters, and symbols—and don't write it down.

9. Keep your credit card close, when shopping or eating out.

Watch how clerks handle your plastic so they don't have a chance to copy it.

10. Mind your own business, and make sure no one else does.

Keep an eye out for anyone who seems a little too interested in your ATM action, and use your free hand to shield the keypad when you enter your PIN. Likewise, don't make sensitive phone calls where other people can overhear you.

11. Secure the home front.

Digging a moat is probably overkill—start small by finding a lockable location in your home where you can store your Social Security card, passport, and all records (including credit card statements) that contain personal information.

More tips! ⟶

MORE **TIPS** ON HOW TO PROTECT YOURSELF...

12. Secure the office front.

After safely stowing your purse and briefcase, look into workplace security procedures for your info. Does the guy who delivers lunch have access to your W-4? He probably shouldn't. Talk to your boss and explain the importance of keeping personal information confidential.

13. Don't give out your SSN.

Just because there's a space for it on the form. Employers, credit grantors and schools may need your Social Security number—but your grocery store's savings club does not. (Are they going to run a credit check before you buy a box of cereal?) When a business asks for it, ask why they need it, what they plan to do with it, and how they will keep it safe. It's your SSN, and you have a right to know.

14. Ask for a safer ID number.

Try not to let businesses use your SSN as an identification number that's printed on every piece of paper you receive. Some businesses—health insurance companies, for instance—may not be willing to give you an alternate number, but it can't hurt to ask. If your Driver's License Number is your SSN, your state government needs to get with the program. You can ask to have it changed.

15. Only carry what you need.

It's one thing to be prepared, but you really aren't going to need your Social Security card when you run out to pick up a gallon of milk. Keep any unessential cards locked up at home.

16. Spring clean your credit cards.

If you aren't regularly using your "Sausage-World" credit card, cancel it. The fewer cards you have, the less you have to keep track of, and the smaller the chances of losing one. Keep organized records of all your credit cards so that you can report theft promptly and thoroughly.

17. Don't put your SSN on your checks.

The less information you give out, the better, so it's a good idea to leave off your phone number too. The same rule applies to résumés: a prospective employer will need your phone number, obviously, but you don't have to provide your SSN and birth date until later in the game.

18. ■ Install a firewall and virus software.

And come on now, why is your credit card number publicly posted on your web page? Seriously though, folks, Internet access leaves you open to identity theft in many thrilling ways. For the full story on internet safety, check out Page 41.

19. ■ Opt out.

Tired of telemarketers who call during dinner? Sick of junk e-mail for products no one would ever want? Opting out means getting your name off these marketing lists and making some of it stop. It isn't entirely an identity theft issue, but if fewer businesses have and sell your data, fewer thieves will be able to find it. Page 62, conveniently, has all you need to know about opting out.

20. ■ Read privacy polices.

Yes, we mean those densely printed, poorly worded slips of paper your bank sends you every year, the ones that all look exactly the same. Yes, read them. Why? Because, dull as they are, they'll tell you what your bank is doing with your personal information, and what you can do to opt out of having that info shared. See Page 60 for some help with this oh-so-boring chore.

BONUS TIP:

Place fraud alerts on your credit reports. This tip somehow escaped from the "what to do once it happens" chapter and ended up in this list. Fortunately, it works here too— but in a very sneaky way. How? Well, fraud alerts tell anyone who orders your report that a crook is doing mean and illegal things with your identity. These alerts also ask credit grantors to give you a ring before giving "you" a new credit account. So, if you place a fraud alert on your own account preemptively—before any fraud has occurred—you'll know right away when a thief applies for credit in your name. See? See? We're smarter than we look, eh? (But be warned: this trick can make it harder for you to get credit when you really want it. See Page 47 for more details.)

Q: SHOULD I GET ID THEFT INSURANCE?

A: PROBABLY NOT.

Okay, the decision is up to you, but keep in mind that no one but the companies selling the insurance recommends this step. That should be a clue. For around $25 to $60 a year, these companies offer identity theft policies to cover the expenses associated with theft—lost wages, mailing and phone charges, and attorney's fees, for instance. While that might sound good at first, the truth is that the maximum coverage for lost wages can be miniscule compared to your salary. And as for legal fees, few victims actually require a lawyer. On top of all that, don't forget that you may already have ID theft coverage as part of your homeowner's insurance. Why pay twice?

The other problem with ID theft insurance is this: it only covers the financial losses, which are only one part of what a victim has to deal with. Identity theft insurance doesn't comfort you when you feel violated, wait on hold for you when you call the credit bureaus, or help you make sense of the complicated and frustrating project of clearing your name. At best, identity theft insurance helps to ease part of your financial burden if you become a victim. At worst, it takes advantage of your fears by selling you a service you don't really need, then lulls you into a false sense of security, and only resolves part of the problem once your identity is stolen. The best insurance is prevention and early detection.

ID theft insurance!

36

A: THE JURY IS STILL OUT.

> With debit card fraud, a thief steals your money and you have to convince the bank to put it back in your account.

The problem is that although your credit card number and your debit card number are both pretty easy to steal, the results can be quite different. With credit card fraud, the thief steals the bank's money, and your job is to prove you don't really owe it. With debit card fraud, the thief steals your money, and you have to convince the bank to put it back into your account. Guess which one's easier? When a thief steals your credit card you'll never pay more than $50 in fraudulent charges. But when it's your debit card, it's possible to lose all the money in your bank account. See Page 56 for more on how to cope if your debit card is stolen.

HOW TO SPOT A SCAM

Wouldn't it be great if the government were working on a bill requiring scams to be labeled like this?

> **SURGEON GENERAL'S WARNING:** THIS OFFER IS A SCAM. PARTICIPATING IN THIS OFFER MAY RESULT IN IDENTITY THEFT, FINANCIAL LOSS, AND FEELINGS OF REGRET AND FOOLISHNESS.

Well, until that legislation takes effect, you'll need to be on your guard. Here are some common scams, and how to deal with them.

"PHISHING" OR THE ACCOUNT MAINTENANCE SCAM

This is the big one, and it works over the phone or through e-mail. Someone claiming to be from a company you have an account with—your bank, online retailer, or Internet provider, for instance—contacts you to "confirm" your account information, i.e., all the information an identity thief can use. Don't. If it's a phone call, double-check that the caller is legit by hanging up and calling them back using a reliable number. (Get the number yourself from the phone book or a billing statement.) If the account maintenance request comes in an e-mail, it's called phishing, and things get even trickier. You'll be asked to click on a link within the e-mail, which will take you to a site that looks exactly like the company's real site. Don't be fooled! There you'll find a form, and if you fill it out, an identity thief gets all your info. So how can you tell if an e-mail like this is a scam? Well, remember that link in the e-mail? It was probably your Internet provider's real address, but here's the diabolical truth: a link can say one thing and take you somewhere else entirely! Even the address bar on your browser can fool you. Thieves buy domain names that are almost exactly identical to the actual site names: www.yourbank.net becomes www.yourbank.com or www.yourbankonline.net. Again, you need to verify this through a separate source. Call the company directly, or type the address you know is theirs into your browser. If you go to the real website, you'll often find a warning about the scam. If not, forward them the fake e-mail so they can alert other customers.

THE NIGERIAN SCAM

This is another popular one, so if you have an e-mail account, you've probably seen it. Here's how it goes: you get an e-mail from "a government representative," usually from Nigeria, asking for your help moving a large amount of money. Often they'll tell you that you were recommended by a "business associate" as the trustworthy type. In return, you get a cut of the money, and your part is easy. All you have to do is provide your bank account number...Yeah, right. Can you guess where this is going?

We fell for it bigtime.

LOTTERY SCAMS

In this tempting scam, you get an e-mail, often from Canada or the Netherlands, saying you've won money in a lottery. To claim the cash, you simply need to verify your identity. Ummm, not to burst your bubble, but if you didn't enter the lottery, it's highly unlikely that you managed to win it. Repeat after us: S-C-A-M.

FREE GIFT SCAMS

You've won an amazing free gift! (Just give us your credit card number for a small shipping and handling fee.) Well, then, it's not really free, now is it? Don't give your credit card number to unsolicited e-mail offers. Don't make us say it again! If you're really tempted by the "free" toy, investigate the company first to make sure it's legitimate. Does it have a phone number you can call to reach a live person? Does the area code match the address of the company? Call the Better Business Bureau where the company is located to get all the dirt.

THE "OLD FRIEND" SCAMS

Someone e-mails you claiming to be a long-lost friend, maybe someone from a chatroom, and asks you some seemingly innocent questions. But remember: Friends don't make friends fill out questionnaires! This is an identity thief trying to weasel info out of you, like your birth date and your interests, which could help them figure out your password. Don't respond.

THE IRS SCAM

If you get an e-mail from the IRS warning you that you have been chosen for an e-audit, and asking you to fill out some forms, keep the following facts in mind: the IRS doesn't perform e-audits, and they don't warn you when they are planning to audit you. Oh, so that's probably another scam, huh?

In short, trust no one. Anyone can sound professional over the phone, and anyone can create an official-looking website. If someone contacts you and asks for information, that's your biggest clue that something's wrong. Investigate thoroughly before you tell anyone anything.

WHO'S WATCHING YOU ON THE WEB?

Identity Theft and the Internet

Not every virus is lurking about your hard drive looking for your SSN, and not every piece of spam you receive is a solicitation from an identity thief. But some of them are. Nine out of ten identity thieves agree that the Internet makes their job a whole lot easier. Read on to find out how you can make it a little harder.

DEFEND YOUR FORTRESS... ER, COMPUTER

1 VIRUS PROTECTION

Viruses—programs written by hackers to mess with your computer—can do any number of unpleasant things, some of which can be quite handy for an identity thief. For instance, a virus could keep track of every key you type, which might include your passwords or your credit card number. The virus then sends that information back to the thief. Virus protection programs search out and destroy these sneaky bits of code, but the software has to know what it's looking for. Update your virus protection software regularly and whenever you receive an alert about a new virus.

2 WINDOWS UPDATES

Despite its many useful capabilities, Windows contains some security loopholes that hackers find and exploit for their own gain. Fortunately, Microsoft is always working to come up with security patches to stop the hackers and thieves. But you've got to install the Microsoft updates if you want to be protected. Update your operating system whenever it tells you to— even if you're in the middle of a particularly important game of Minesweeper.

3 FIREWALLS

When you venture out for a stroll in cyberspace, you use the front door: your browser. What you probably don't realize is that there are thousands of other doors, windows, and ventilation shafts (ports, if you want to get all technical) through which your computer can be accessed. If you leave all of those entrances wide open, you're just begging an identity thief to get in there and steal information. Firewall software protects your computer by locking the extra doors and windows. This is especially important if you have a high-speed Internet connection that's always on.

41

JUST SAY NO...

TO DOWNLOADS FROM STRANGERS

You're surfing the web and a window pops up. You don't really read it (who has time to read all those boring gray windows?) but you click "yes" to make it go away. Congratulations…you just downloaded a program. It may, of course, be a friendly harmless program. Then again it also might be a mean sneaky program that changes your firewall settings and snoops around your computer for personal information. Many of these programs, known as "spyware," really do perform useful functions while also doing less desirable things just under your radar. The point is, you really don't know. Once you let a program onto your computer, it can do just about anything, and its movements can be very hard to detect.

The solution? Click "no" instead of "yes." Your browser usually has to ask you if you want to download, so read those boring gray boxes carefully, and choose your downloads wisely. If you've downloaded a lot of free software and can't seem to make it go away, you may want to get "spy-killer" or "ad-killer" software, which is designed to find and delete all your spyware.

PRACTICE SAFE SHOPPING

Ahh, Internet shopping.
No lines, no crowded parking lot...you don't even have to put on a shirt.
And neither does an identity thief before he hacks into a web merchant's
database and steals your credit card number.

☐ Shop from secure sites, which will encrypt your order info—including your credit card number—before sending it to a merchant. To make sure your connection is secure, look for "https://" at the beginning of the URL in the address bar (it's the "s" that's important). Also check for a little picture of a padlock or an unbroken key in the bottom right hand corner of your browser.

☐ Use only one credit card for all online pur chases. It's easier to keep track that way if fraudulent charges occur. The only exception: If you're shopping on a department store's web site and you have their store credit card, use that instead.

☐ Read privacy policies. Secure ordering only protects your information en route. A privacy policy should tell you if the company is going to store and use your information safely once it arrives.

☐ Shop at sites you know. If you aren't sure about a site, do a little research before you divulge your digits.

☐ Look for privacy seals—like BBBOnline, TRUSTe, or VeriSign—on the sites where you shop. These colorful little logos, usually located at the bottom of a homepage, certify that the company adheres to certain privacy and security guidelines. Click on the seal to make sure it's genuine, and to find out exactly what its placement on the site means.

☐ Shop with a credit card—not a debit card. If a thief intercepts your credit card number and runs up charges, federal law limits your liability to $50 per card. If the same thing happens with your debit card, you can lose $500 or more.

☐ Keep detailed records of your online purchases in case anything goes wrong.

☐ Log off after using public Internet terminals, and, if possible, save your shopping for your home computer.

☐ Use special software to wipe your hard drive clean before chucking your old computer.

HOW TO

COPE

WHEN THE #1 CRIME HAPPENS TO YOU

Typically, when a crime is committed, the police take care of things. It's what they're paid to do. When the crime is identity theft, however, you get to take on your case all by yourself. And cleaning up the mess a thief made is a huge chore.

In more complicated identity theft cases, when multiple new accounts are opened in your name, restoring your credit can take tons of time, money, and dedication. You might even have to take time off work to focus on the project, which can take months upon frustrating months to complete.

Emotional Impact

Bottom line: It's not fun, and it's not fair. It's okay, healthy even, to be furious about it. You'll probably feel some combination of anger, hurt, helplessness, dread, even betrayal if the thief is someone you know, and these kinds of feelings are totally to be expected. So talk to a friend, punch a pillow, or maybe even talk to a professional. And then try to look at your new full-time job—restoring your credit—as the perfect way to keep your mind off all those messy emotions!

THREE BIG STEPS TO DEALING WITH ID THEFT

spent months fixing it!

STEP ONE:

Contact the Credit Bureau Fraud Departments

First things first, you need to get a fraud alert and a victim statement placed on your credit reports. The fraud alert is a signal to businesses that someone's been doing nasty things with your identity. It will prompt a credit card company to be a little more careful next time "you" apply for a card. The victim statement is a word from you, and you want it to go something like this: "My identifying information has been used to commit fraud. Please call me at [insert your phone number] to verify all applications." (Please note that fraud alerts and victim statements will make it more complicated for you to apply for credit—that's the point! If it's a hassle for you, it should be impossible for a thief.)

To make things less complicated, for once, one phone call will do the job of notifying all three credit bureaus. Call any one of the fraud departments listed below, tell them you are a victim, and ask for a fraud alert and victim statement. Once one credit bureau has your info, they'll bring the other two up to speed. Fraud alerts will be placed on all of your credit reports, and you'll receive a complimentary copy of each report. (When these arrive, check them carefully to make sure you're aware of all the fraud that's occurred.)

The "one-call" system only places fraud alerts and victim statements on your report for a short period of time— usually three to twelve months. To make it more permanent, seven years of permanence to be exact, you'll need to write to each credit bureau separately and request a renewal.

Be careful, however: if your situation was minor and easily cleared up, you may not want a fraud alert on your record for seven long years, since the alert will make it harder for you to get credit when you need it.

Also, keep in mind that credit grantors abide by fraud alerts and victim statements on a voluntary basis only. So far, no law requires that they do so. This means it may still be possible for a thief to open accounts in your name, so continue to order your credit reports every three months for at least a year.

CREDIT BUREAU FRAUD DEPARTMENTS

Equifax
www.equifax.com
800-525-6285
P.O. Box 105069
Atlanta, GA 30398

Experian
www.experian.com
888-397-3742
P.O. Box 9532
Allen, TX 75013

TransUnion
www.transunion.com
800-680-7289
Fraud Victim Assistance Department
P.O. Box 6790
Fullerton, CA 92834

STEP TWO:

Shut Down
All Compromised Accounts

This means you pull the plug on both types of accounts—your old accounts the thief was misusing, plus any new accounts the thief opened in your name. Don't forget that this could include credit card companies or service providers like your phone, ISP, or utilities. When you reopen your accounts, make sure you have a new account number, and guard it with a new password. (Use something only you could know—which is kind of the point of a password.) You can protect your rep by asking the creditor to classify the old account as "closed at customer's request." The other option—"Card lost or stolen"—can make you look careless, even though we know it wasn't your fault.

If your ATM or debit card was stolen, the procedure is pretty much the same. Report the theft ASAP, cancel the card, and get a new card with a new PIN. If the identity thief stole checks, call the bank and stop payment on any outstanding checks you didn't write. Then contact the check verification services so they can tell their retailers not to accept checks from the thief. For current phone numbers go to www.realuguides.com.

Closing accounts that were yours to begin with is pretty easy. The hard part is getting rid of the charges that you didn't make, and closing accounts you didn't ever open. Ask to speak to the fraud department of the bank, retailer, or credit card company, and find out what forms you need to dispute fraudulent charges and accounts. You may be able to use the ID Theft Affidavit—a standard form available online. (See Page 53 for more info.) Or you may need to use the company's own forms. For now, go on record about everything you are disputing, and have the forms you need sent to you. Be sure to follow these calls up in writing to make things extra-official. If you're dealing with a new account, get as much documentation about it as you can, such as a copy of the application used to open the account and transactions records. If the creditor won't give up the goods on your thief's account, it's probably because of their security policy—take a moment to laugh at the irony. Then keep trying. Getting the cops involved, or at least getting a police report, can help.

STEP THREE:

File a Police Report

Throughout this process, you're going to be faced by skepticism. Companies will want some kind of proof that you really are a victim, and not just some jerk trying to get out of paying your debts. A police report is the best proof you can offer, because creditors assume you wouldn't file a police report unless you really meant it. (You wouldn't, right? Don't make us come over there!)

The problem is, it can sometimes be difficult to get the police to take you seriously, so you'll have to be persistent. Explain that without a police report you have no way to stop the theft and repair your credit. Provide the police with copies of any documentation you already have, like your credit report, debt collection letters, or the ID Theft Affidavit. If the local police still refuse to help you, go to the county police, and then try the state police. If they say identity theft isn't a crime in your state, ask to file a Miscellaneous Incident Report instead.

They may even catch the thief!

When you file the report, be certain that it lists every instance of fraud committed with your identifying information. And make sure you get a copy of it, so you can send copies to creditors. (When you do that, it's also helpful to include the phone number of the investigating officer.) If you absolutely can't get a copy of the police report, get the report number, and ask for a letter stating that the report couldn't be given to you.

Paperwork, Paperwork, Paperwork.

How To Stay Organized and Be Effective

Because of the size of the task in front of you, keeping good records and staying organized are essential.

If tying a string around your finger is your only system for keeping track of stuff, your hands will soon be so knotted with string that you won't be able to dial the phone. Maybe you should find a new system, before you cause a national string shortage. Try these strategies:

☐ Send all letters certified mail, return receipt requested. This gives you a record of when you sent something and when it was received.

☐ If you want to play it extra safe, ask the people you speak to for written confirmation of your conversations. If they refuse, you can write to them (certified mail, return receipt requested, of course), list what was said, and ask them to write back if anything is incorrect. If they don't reply, that can serve as your confirmation.

Did we mention paperwork?

- Keep copies of all letters and forms you send.

- Keep the originals of every piece of paper you didn't generate—like police reports, credit reports, and all letters you receive.

- Hang on to all your old files, even after you think the ordeal is over. If anything comes back to haunt you, Murphy's Law says you'll need that one piece of paper you threw out.

- Always have a plan of action. List what you need to accomplish, how you can do it, and whom you'll need to speak to.

- Keep a log of everything you do—every letter you send and receive, every phone call you make. (You can leave out the bathroom breaks.)

- Keep records of all phone conversations: names of the persons you spoke to, their titles, and phone numbers; what you discussed; what they agreed to and when; what they need from you and when.

- Use a filing system that will give you ready access to everything you need. (That pile in the corner is not a filing system.)

- Follow up all phone calls and face-to-face conversations in writing. The people you talk to at credit card companies and law enforcement agencies may deal with hundreds of calls just like yours every day. Even if they sound reassuring on the phone, they might forget you the moment they hang up, and it's only your word against theirs that you ever spoke. Putting things in writing will jog some memories and give you proof that the communication actually occurred.

- You may want to keep track of your costs, in case your thief is caught. Your chances of getting some money back are much better if you keep a log and save your receipts. Eligible expenditures may include: phone calls, postage, mileage, legal assistance, notarizing, court costs for documentation, time lost from work, organizational and reference materials, and personal assistance like a babysitter or an accountant.

Murphy's Law says you'll need that one piece of paper you threw out.

MAKE YOUR PHONE CALLS **COUNT**

- ☐ Decide before you call what your goal is—what you need to know or accomplish—and plan what you're going to ask or say to achieve that goal.

- ☐ Listen when the other person is talking, and take notes.

- ☐ Be stubborn. If the person you are speaking to can't help you, ask to talk to someone who can.

- ☐ Don't hang up till you're satisfied and understand everything.

BE STUBBORN. If the person you are speaking to can't help you, ask to talk to someone who can.

FILE A COMPLAINT WITH THE **FTC**

In addition to all the other paperwork, it's a good idea to call the Federal Trade Commission to report the crime.

Why? Although they can't catch the bad guys for you, they maintain a database of information for law enforcement types, who just might be able to track down your thief. Also, the FTC uses the information they gather to learn more about identity theft, which helps them help victims like you. These guys are on your side, so give them a call and tell your story.

To notify the FTC, call 1-877-IDTHEFT.

THE ID THEFT AFFIDAVIT

This handy tool is a standard form—a three-page master key to identity theft repair. It can help you begin to fix up your credit, especially if you are unable to get a police report. Many companies accept the ID Theft Affidavit as a fraud dispute form, which is nice unless you really like endless paperwork. (Some companies still want you to fill out their own forms, so check first.) How do you get it? Luckily, it's just a few clicks and one easy download away. Check out www.realuguides.com for details.

THE REST OF

If you followed the first three steps, you've probably stopped the thief from committing further fraud, but there's still plenty to do. Your credit report is a joke, and not a very funny one. Plus there are probably debt collectors lurking in the bushes outside your front door. Here's how to deal with the rest of the mess.

1.CORRECTING YOUR CREDIT REPORT

What you should know:

By law, both the credit bureaus and the information providers—the credit grantors who give them information about you—are responsible for correcting inaccuracies on your credit report. To make sure this really happens, attack on both fronts: contact the credit bureaus and the information providers.

What you should do:

First call each of the three credit bureaus, and follow up in writing. Your letter should be detailed and specific: identify each item you are disputing by the name of the company and the type of account; for each explain why you are disputing it, and ask that it be corrected or deleted. Include any supporting documentation that you have, such as the Identity Theft Affidavit and police report. If you already have documents from the credit grantor agreeing that the charge or account is fraudulent, you definitely want to include copies.

What they have to do:

The credit bureau gets 30-45 days to investigate your case. (If they think it's frivolous and aren't going to bother with it, they have to let you know within five days.) The credit bureau then sends you a written report of the outcome. If the information provider—the store or bank where the fraud occurred—determines that your claim is true and the items you are disputing are in fact incorrect, they are responsible for notifying all the credit bureaus they work with. The credit bureaus must, by law, correct or delete all the inaccurate information, including all fraudulent accounts and charges, and any fraudulent inquiries.

What you should do then:

Make sure everyone knows! If you ask, the credit bureaus must send corrected copies of your report to any business who has received it in the last 6 months, and to any employers who've had a peek in the last two years. If there are still problems with your credit report, you can ask to have a statement added to it to explain your side of the story.

THE MESS

2. CLEARING UP CREDIT FRAUD

What you should know:

In most cases, your liability when a thief steals your credit card and hits the mall is limited to $50 per card. (Some banks and card companies offer $0 liability—an even better deal.) To take advantage of this deal, though, you need to act promptly.

What you should do:

From the time you receive the credit card statement listing the fraudulent charge, you have 60 days to dispute that charge. This is true even if the thief changed your address and you never actually received the statement listing the $5,000 he spent on Elvis memorabilia—so keep track of your billing cycles! When you write to the credit card company, include your name, account number, and a detailed list of the fraudulent charges, including the date and the amount. Make sure you address the letter to the billing inquiry department, and—all together now—send it certified mail, return receipt requested. Don't forget to include all relevant documentation.

What they have to do:

The credit card company has 30 days to let you know they received your letter, and must resolve the dispute within two billing cycles (90 days max).

What you should do then:

It's important to get a letter from the credit card company which says that the charges were fraudulent and that they have been removed. Hang on to the original of this letter like it's a winning lottery ticket—and include a copy whenever you write to credit bureaus or debt collectors. You'll want to get the same kind of letter when you shut down bad credit accounts that the thief opened in your name.

starting over

3. DEALING WITH DEBIT CARDS

What you should know:

Your liability when money is stolen from your bank account, with a debit or ATM card for instance, all depends on how quickly you report the theft, so you've got to act fast...really fast. If you report it within 2 days, you'll only lose $50. If it takes more than 2 days, but under 60, you can lose up to $500, and if it takes you more than 60 days to report the theft, you can lose all the money you had in your account. (Some debit card companies voluntarily cap your liability at $50, same as a credit card. Check with your financial institution to find out their policy.)

What you should do:

Take all the same steps you would take if this were a credit card fraud. In this case, because timing is everything, it's even more important to send the letter certified mail, return receipt requested.

What they have to do:

You had to act fast, so it's only fair that they do too. Your financial institution has ten days to investigate your case, three days to notify you of the result, and one day to fix the error once they've finished investigating. If it takes longer than that, they must return the money to your account while they investigate, for up to 45 days. They'll want that money back if they find out you really did spend it, but they have to notify you in writing first.

What you should do then:

See the section on what to do for credit card fraud, on Page 55. Do likewise.

I can't take it anymore!

4. GETTING RID OF THE DEBT COLLECTORS

What you should know:

The law says that if you write and ask a debt collector to leave you alone, they have to. Well that was easy! After that, all they can do is contact you to tell you they aren't going to contact you anymore (which is kind of amusing), or to tell you that they're going to take some specific action.

What you should do:

On the off chance that that specific action might be something unpleasant, it's best to write to the collection agency—within 30 days of receiving their notice—and tell them that you don't actually owe the debt. Explain about the identity theft, and include any documentation.

What they have to do:

In order to keep bugging you, they need to provide you with proof that you do owe the debt. Often, your debt will just be referred back to the original creditor.

What you should do then:

Getting rid of debt collectors doesn't get rid of the debt. You still need to contact the creditor and deal with that little detail. See "Clearing Up Credit Fraud" on Page 55.

But wait, there's more...

If your identity theft involved the mail in any way, tell the U.S. Postal Inspection Service. Call your local post office or visit www.usps.gov/websites/depart/inspect.

Did the thief get a driver's license in your name? Talk to your local DMV.

Got passport problems? The United States Department of State can field that one. Go to www.travel.state.gov/passport_services.html or look up their local office in the Blue Pages.

Did that jerk invest, file for bankruptcy, take out a student loan, get phone service, or file tax returns in your name?

Do you suddenly have a criminal record that you're pretty darn sure isn't yours?

Check out www.realuguides.com for more useful website links.

PAST DUE

LET'S FIX

Dropping your dough with companies that have good privacy and security practices not only protects you, it also sends the message that it matters to you whether they take good care of your information.

THIS MESS

If you're ready to make a choice and make a change...here's all you need to know about reading privacy policies, opting out, and telling your lawmakers what's up.

Banks and credit card companies lose big bucks from identity theft—$18,000 per incident, on average—yet they aren't doing all they could to prevent it. Because they can write the money off as bad debt, it's been cheaper so far not to invest in prevention measures. That doesn't help you much, does it? To make your information safer, companies need:

- tighter security against hackers and thieves;

- better screening processes for job applicants and restricted employee access to sensitive information;

- effective systems for verifying identity and detecting fraudulent applications.

So what can you do to press for these practices? For one thing, money talks. As a consumer, your leverage comes from where you choose to spend your money. Dropping your dough with companies that have good privacy and security practices not only protects you, it also sends the message that it matters to you whether they take good care of your information. What else can you do? Turn the page and find out.

Write a letter to your lawmakers!

HOW TO READ
A PRIVACY POLICY

The average American household gets between 10 and 15 privacy notices a year in the mail, and on top of that nearly every shopping website has one, too.

Before you open a bank account or order online, you should find out what's going to happen to your personal information. A privacy policy will tell you what personal information a business collects, and how they collect it. (On the Internet, look for a section on cookies, too.) You can also learn how they use your information, who they share it with, and what opt-out options you have for limiting how your personal ID is collected and distributed. Look very closely at what the company does to ensure that your information is safely transmitted and stored.

"Oh great, another privacy notice."

GLOSSARY OF PRIVACY POLICY TERMS

Confused by big words (or small ones you haven't seen before)? Don't worry, we won't tell. When you read privacy policies, you'll run into a lot of corporate-speak. Here's a handy glossary to help you decode it all.

Affiliate—A company that is owned by your company,*or by the same "parent" company.

Cookie—A small file stored on your hard drive by a website you visit, used to identify you when you return to that site.

Creditworthiness—Information such as your credit score and bill-paying history that can point to the risk in giving you credit.

Joint Marketer—A company that has made a deal with your company, allowing them to sell you something. For example, a company that offers financial planning might strike a deal with your bank to try to sell their service to the bank's customers. (There is no law allowing you to opt-out of having your information shared with joint marketers.)

Non-affiliated third party—A completely separate company, not an affiliate of your company.

Personally Identifiable Information (a.k.a. Nonpublic Personal Information)—Information that may be used to uniquely identify you, such as your name, Social Security number, credit card number, or bank account number.

Publicly Available Information—Stuff about you that anyone could find out, like your phone number.

Service Provider (a.k.a. Agent)—A company hired by your company to perform a specific function, such as shipping or billing.

Transaction & Experience Information—The details about where you spend your money (for example, the kind of information listed on your credit card statement).

(*The company that wrote the privacy policy)

61

HOW TO OPT ∅ OUT

Should you opt out? That depends on how much you like getting junk mail. But remember this—the fewer times your personal information is copied and shared, the smaller the chances that an identity thief will find it.

Financial institutions are required by law to tell you what information they collect and how they use it. They also have to give you the option to opt-out of information-sharing with non-affiliated third-parties. (See the glossary again if you're lost already!)

Specific businesses, like your bank or a web merchant, should tell you about your opt-out choices in their privacy policies, but unless you live in a shack and don't tend to get out much, your information is already out there somewhere. Here's all the contact info you need to stop the spread.

Pre-screened Credit Offers

Call: 1-888-5-OPTOUT (567-8688)

Marketing Lists

(To take your name off lists generated by credit bureaus.) Write:

Equifax, Inc.
Options
PO Box 740123
Atlanta, GA 30374

Experian
Consumer Opt-Out
701 Experian Parkway
Allen, TX 75013

TransUnion
Marketing List Opt Out
PO Box 97328
Jackson, MS 39288

Telemarketing

(To stop calls from companies registered with the Direct Marketing Association.) Write or go online:

Direct Marketing Association
Telephone Preference Service
PO Box 1559
Carmel, NY 10512
www.the-dma.org/consumers/offtelephonelist.html

National Do Not Call Registry

Call or go online:
1-888-382-1222
www.donotcall.gov

State Do Not Call Lists

Go to: www.ftc.gov/donotcall

Direct Mail Marketing

(To stop mail from companies registered with the Direct Marketing Association.) Write or go online:

Direct Marketing Association
Mail Preference Service
PO Box 643
Carmel, NY 10512
www.the-dma.org/consumers/offmailinglist.html

Spam

(To stop e-mail from companies registered with the Direct Marketing Association.)
Online: www.the-dma.org/consumers/offemaillist.html

THERE OUGHTTA BE A LAW...

How to Lobby Congress for More Protection

In an ideal world, businesses and government agencies would voluntarily do all they could to prevent identity theft and help victims out. In the real world, we need to pass some laws to prevent identity theft—like requiring businesses to shred sensitive documents before tossing them. We also need laws to help people if they become victims—like requiring the police to take a report of the crime. If you want to research current laws, find out what laws are being considered, and learn how to contact your very own elected officials, the Internet is your new best friend. Visit www.realuguides.com for a list of links to get you started, plus some tips on how to communicate effectively with the people in power.

More laws on identity theft need to be passed

MORE REAL U...
CHECK OUT THESE OTHER REAL U GUIDES!

PLANNING FOR COLLEGE

With a timeline for high school freshmen, sophomores, juniors, and seniors, this guide takes you step by step through the whole college selection and application process. Includes a clear and concise overview of financial aid, and much more.

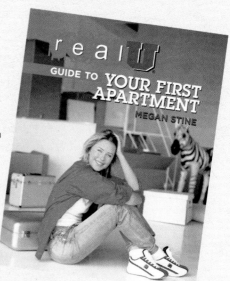

YOUR FIRST APARTMENT

Everything you need to know about moving out of the house and into your first apartment, including how to deal with landlords, how to dump your roommate, and much more!

PLUS LIVING ON YOUR OWN

So you've finally moved into your first apartment. Now what? Plunge into real life with a safety net. If you can't cook, always shrink your socks, and have no idea where to find your stove's pilot light, this is the guide for you.

BUYING YOUR FIRST CAR

Don't get burned on the first big purchase you make. Find out how to get the best financing, how to avoid the latest scam tactics, whether to buy extended warranties, and more.